ESCAPE FROM THE PLANET CROUTON

Poems by Wayne F. Burke

Luchador Press
Big Tuna, TX

Copyright © Wayne F. Burke, 2019
First Edition1 3 5 7 9 10 8 6 4 2
ISBN: 978-1-950380-78-7
LCCN: 2019955709

Design, edits and layout: El Dopa
Title page image: Wayne F. Burke
Author photo: Wayne F. Burke
All rights reserved. No part of this publication may be reproduced or transmitted in any form or by any means, electronic or mechanical, including photocopying, recording or by info retrieval system, without prior written permission from the author.

The author would like to thank as well as acknowledge the following publications where some of these poems first appeared: *Unlikely Stories Mark V, The Daily Dope Fiend, Alien Buddha Press, Rust Belt Review, The Stray Branch, 13 Myna Birds, Piker Press, The Beatnik Cowboy, 300K A Poetry Anthology, The Torrid Review, The Conclusion, Rye Whiskey Review, Drinkers Only, Haikuniverse, Horror Sleaze Trash, Mad Swirl*, and *The Five-Two.*

TABLE OF CONTENTS

1.

Polio / 1

Palmer Method / 2

TB / 3

Witness / 4

Farm / 6

Runaway / 8

100 Pounds / 9

M-80 / 10

Prepositioned / 12

2.

Highway / 15

Beaver / 17

Dee-Wee / 19

Hot Ticket / 20

Irate / 21

Tattoo / 22

3.

Van Gogh / 24

Schwittzers / 27

Pollock / 28

Al Dugan / 30

Poets / 32

The Track / 34

4.

Dick at the Fair / 37

Dick Puts the Plug in the Jug / 39

Rabies / 41

The Human Race / 43

Ha / 44

Another Day / 46

5.

I Write For the Factory Workers / 49

Hypnopompic / 51

Excavation / 53

Reunion / 55

Nap / 57

1st Book / 58

Glucose / 59

6.

Loopy / 63

Raindrops / 64

The Old Lady / 65

Sunrise at the Sunset / 68

Spit / 69

7.

RNA / 73

Gulf Coast / 74

Greatness / 76

Soups & Greens / 78

Dublin / 79

One Dog Then / 80

Budapest / 81

Eye / 82

Last Bus / 83

Meanwhile / 84

8.

Doorknob / 87

In Case of Emergency / 89

Shut-Off / 91

It a Lie / 93

Dedicated to my sister, who read my books:
Lynn Ann Burke-LaCasse, 1950-2016. And my cousin,
Andrew Kalisz, 1952-2019, who read my stories.

1.

1.

the clapboard Inn

my grandfather owned—

marble in the dream

Polio

Charlie Baguette's brother Davy
who had polio
used a crutch;
he stood by the porch and
played 45s on a record player
as Charlie and I stripped the
thorny pulp off horse chestnuts
and put the ebony nuts into
a brown shopping bag
and threw the nuts that night
Halloween
at the Camel's house across the street
until cops came with their shining blue
light and
we ran
into the backyard shadows--
the Camel's thought themselves better
than us, and were mean too
like the German Shepard they kept chained
in their yard:
Davy played Running Bear
Loved Little White Dove
(with a love that never died).
It was the beat of the tom-tom
had set Charlie and me on the
war-path.

Palmer Method

we studied penmanship in school,
wrote long lines of 'c's
like waves coming to shore
and 'e's like little heads;
Miss Good, 3rd grade teacher
blind as a bat
and batty
beat our knuckles with a ruler
then loved us up later
with smothering lilac-scented
flesh; she
lived alone in a brick house
wore a red dress
or else green
one day she broke her yardstick
over the shoulders of Jimmy
and the broken half clattered to the floor
and we all laughed
and laughed.

TB

when they told me my grandmother
died in the hospital
in Northampton of
tuberculosis
I asked, *what is that?*
and my Uncle told me shut-up
I did not need to know everything
and I wondered why not
but did not ask
because
did not want a back-handed slap;
I had not seen the old lady in years,
had heard her name only in
whispered conversations--
*hey, isn't Northampton the
nuthouse?*
Grandma shoved me toward the door;
the collar of my shirt choked me
and my tie strangled like a noose:
it is not a nuthouse, she said
it is a hospital.

Witness

Bowling For Dollars on TV
Saturday afternoon
my feet up on the cushioned chair
sound of the ball rolling down the
lane,
a knock at the door
I run to answer
two women
one big one small
hello, little boy, are your parents home?
My Uncle comes into the hallway,
shoves me aside,
he wears green gas station pants
cuffs dragging the floor
what do you want? he growls.
The big woman talks.
I sniff the musty odor of the
doily stretched across a side window—
we are not interested!
The door slams shut,
the women walk across the road;
Grandma, from the kitchen
asks, *who were they?*
Jehovah's Witnesses.
She wipes her hands on an apron:
did you have to be so rough?

Yes! You know they would not fight in the war!
Uncle stomps into the dining room,
peeks through the blinds.
Leno Decensi is talking to them!
Wasn't he in the navy, Ma?
Smooth roll of a bowling ball
splatters pins in all directions.

Farm

He he, ha ha
they are coming
to take me away
the song played
on the car radio
the ride home
from Sand Springs
the aqua blue pool
in Williamstown
the *Village Beautiful*
Gramp with a smile
on his face ha ha
he he his hand on the
steering wheel of the
big Buick; I wondered
what he found funny,
I hung my arm out the
car window and
Grandma, in the middle
crabbed, *you want to*
get your arm cut off?
and I said *yes* but
pulled it back in;
I heard my brother and
cousin in the rear both
shout *beaver!* after

spotting a station wagon
from the back window
(first to ten *beavers* won)
it was a half hour drive
home
to the funny farm
in
Adams.

Runaway

I ran away from home
seven years old
walked out of the house and
down the road
along cracked and gouged sidewalk
a quarter mile to the lime kiln
loud waterfall-roar of machinery
white dust in the air and
smoky white buildings,
trucks banging along the highway
over railroad tracks…
I came to a hill where the
road dropped to a dark canyon,
a long channel of shadow
between rows of brown brick tenement blocks—
a German Shepard, chained to a rail
atop a cement landing
barked and slobbered and
I got scared,
turned around and
walked back to the
home I had run from…
Nobody there knew I had been gone.

100 Pounds

my Uncle the fat mama's boy
collapsed one night
on the porch
and was taken to the hospital with
heart attack
and
afterward went on a diet
began to exercise
lost a hundred pounds
and went unrecognized by
those who knew him,
and then
aged 35
he got married and
moved out of the house
and
I was free
of his rules that changed like his moods,
of his back-handed slaps,
of the stench of his B.O.,
of the stare of his dark eyes,
brown
not blue
like mine.

M-80

was an explosive
a firecracker
shaped like a shot glass;
Maloney dropped one on the
Camel's doorstep
BAWAM
we ran
up into the field and
lay in the tall grass
like deer
as the cops searched
with spotlights
until wise-mouth Little Abbo
yelled *we're over here!*
and we ran
while the spotlight flickered—
we regathered on the
old lime kiln road and
descended upon Brody's garden,
kicked to shreds his tomato plants
trampled his cucumbers,
crossed the highway and
surrounded the Salerno's house and
rapped on the windows until
Mr. Salerno, who taught music at the
Junior High, ran out and
shouted *what did we ever do to you?*

The cops chased us into the cow pasture
where we hid in shadow
beneath the mountain until
the coast clear
and the moon-light white on the
back road where
we dilly-dallied long enough
to open a car hood and
tear all the hoses and wires out…
It had been a big night.
The stars bright,
shining as if for us
alone:
six monthis later the Salerno's moved
and Brody black-topped his yard
and that car
I never did hear if
they ever got it
started.

Prepositioned

To, is, and, if, but
the prepositions of grammar school
rendition,
how about *then* and *than* and
was and *were?*
The teacher explained usage
but I did not get it;
got *your* and *you're*
their and *they're* but
not then/than
or was/were
I do not think the
teacher knew
more about it
then/than I did
but she the one
flunked me,
told my grandparents
I was/were slow
which was/were news to
them/there and
suggested I be put into
special class
which
back in them/thar days
was/were called
retarded.

2.

they say the sun
will die—
it a lie
don't believe it

Highway

my Uncle the Mayor
got me a job
with the highway department
for the summer,
until I returned to college;
Ken and George and me
in an orange truck
Ken drove,
he was a smile-er
a *good morning* of white teeth
had pleats in his slacks
and did not like to get dirty;
George sat in the truck
during coffee break
and drank half a pint
(the other half at lunch)
we stopped at pot-holes,
got out,
I shoveled the sweet acrid-smelling
hot tar
then tamped the stuff down
and rolled it…
One afternoon on a desolate stretch of road
I looked up
at a Cadillac passing
and recognized the girl in the
passenger seat,

one of my classmates
and I waved
but she
stared right through me
as if
I were invisible,
or else
she was.

Beaver

I talked my way into a job
at HAROLD'S Gulf station
on the corner
the blue and orange sign and
Harold
shaped like Humpty-Dumpty
sat in an egg-shell white office
smoking cigars and
barking orders at
all the King's Men, Mike
the other attendant and
me, hungover every morning
I sweated through my GULF station shirt by
noon when
I left, went to the park and
laid down…
One day Harold called me into the office
told me I had B.O. and
that customers complained
and that I should do something about it,
OK Harold, I will, I said
but never did
because
what was I suppose to do:
give up drinking?
I stayed in the back of the garage where
it was shady and

the sun did not hurt my eyes as much,
where the car noises hurt my ears
less;
Mike got pissed because had to do my work,
I watched for beavers whenever I washed a car windshield—
beavers and lunch the only good parts of the
job.

Dee-Wee

the plumber fixed the sink
plugged with the life
I live
here
on Planet Crouton
in an a.p.t.
with the shades drawn
and door locked
on the 2nd floor
of a house
on a back street
in a town
some people avoid
and you should too
unless
you want to look me up
I am in the phone book
Wayne F not
Wayne H
some other jerk
got a Dee-Wee
reported by the
newspaper
and the people at work
thought that he
was me.

Hot Ticket

bombing along at 75 mph
in a 50 mph zone
the BMW humming
through
dark countryside,
brake lights in my rear view mirror
oh SHIT
headlights like yellow eyes
pretty blue lights...
hello there, I am officer—
a copette, young, pale-faced
hair pulled back
I hand her the relevant documents,
all legal (even the windshield sticker,
she glimpses) and
I wait
and wait
until her shadow shows
and a white hand appears
holding a pink ticket—
thanks a lot,
drive safe, now.
I park the ticket in the glove box
and she follows me
for fifteen minutes
of *safe* driving.

Irate

in the park
a guy screams
and screams
into a cell phone
and everyone is
relieved
when the guy
finally leaves
but then he
returns
and becomes so upset
he tells *Heather*
to get fucked
and slams the phone
down and
everyone is glad
not to have to listen
to more of his
shit-fit
but then he picks the
phone up
and redials
and begins
again
to make
the nice Spring day
unpleasant
for everyone,
especially Heather.

Tattoo

I got fired because
I come to work
drunk
the boss man says
but I never
not really
ever
just high
from beers at Happy Hour
the pub across the street
but he says I am done
and when I become righteous
pissed
he pulls up his sleeve and
shows me numbers
tattooed to his flesh
from when he was in a camp
in Poland where
he says
he learned what suffering was…
I do not care about
his suffering
only mine
and know
that out on the city streets
and broke
I will soon be tattooed
too.

3.

busy

all

morning

watching

the

clouds

Van Gogh

was a restless kid
his mother a cold
fish
his father, a parson
of respectability;
Vincent was sent to boarding school
he liked home better
and kept returning
like a bad penny
nobody could stand his moodiness
for long
his parents kicked him out
he became a tin Jesus
and went to suffer
with the miners
who thought him a fool
he started to make pictures
after his brother began to pay him
a salary
his parents tried to have him
committed
he moved with the speed and
confusion of
a young Rimbaud
who went to Paris too
like Vincent,
two years in Montmartre
with Theo

before he blew town
for Arles
in the South
16 hours by train
a yellow house
blue moods
and Gauguin
too cool a cat
watched the breakdown
that had been coming
since Brabant
the nut house beckoned
the starry night
the therapeutic baths
the news from Paris and
the Netherlands
and the paint
the paint
on canvases
and the light
lambent
bright
yellow as a heaven
ever could be
purple
in majesty
blue fathoms of
sea
and sky
and twinkling eyes
for posterity…

Then escape from the loony bin
to Auvers
where the stars went out for Vincent,
where Gachet the Alienist
magician
without magic
played his bit part…
Vincent's new door-sized
canvases
like portals so
vast
and deep
with emptiness
nothing could fill them
but
eternity.

Schwittzers

never missed with
his scraps of torn paper
reordered
into little worlds;
theater ticket stubs, doilies, bank notes
cigar wrappers
exquisitely
balanced and
layered—
chaos captured,
banality beautified—
Merz
not *merde.*

Pollock

came out of the West
a mamma's boy who
hung-on apron strings
never cut
he became a child of
the alcoholic NYC night
his brothers took care of him
as did Benton's wife
(and the W.P.A.)
and other women who
mothered him
and then his wife
who thought he could do no wrong
she promoted him
and he became
phenomenon
perhaps the greatest painter
in America
sneered LIFE magazine
perhaps not
he did not know
himself
chump or champ
after all the drips
had dried
he could not break through
again

to anything nearly creative
as those colorful splatters
he went black & white
then figurative
again
and ever deeper into frustration
and a public-suicide trip
(no one called him on his shit)
that finally succeeded
at sixty mph
the final splatter
(he took someone with him,
he never could stand to be alone)
they buried him six feet under
then pulled a huge boulder over
so that
he could not crawl back up.

Al Dugan (1923-2003)

In a corner of the
bathroom
he stood drinking from
a can of Budweiser
he shoved
into his valise
as I entered;
I followed the stench of his B.O.,
his brick-red face,
his corduroy jacket with
elbow patches,
up the corridor to the
classroom
where he argued with the regular professor
over the merit of Joyce's poetry
(Al thought excellent)
and later
that night
Mahoney my asshole poetry buddy
and me
went up to his suite
and Al, Mahoney, and me
got drunk and
I shouted *long live Henry Miller!*
and Al asked
had I ever read Miller's essay
on money?

And I said *no* and
after that
kept my mouth shut
and listened
as Dugan and Mahoney rapped
back and forth
like the pot pipe being passed
and
at some point
Al brought out a poetry manuscript
given him by the college's poetry professor
whom Mahoney called *a lousy Hebe,*
to which Dugan said, *my wife is Jewish*
and Mahoney said *I did not know*
and shortly after that
I blacked-out and
when I came-to
remembered nothing else of the
night except
that Mahoney and Al
thick as thieves,
had agreed that the
manuscript
was *shit.*

Poets

Steinman from Gross Pointe, Michigan
told everyone who asked
that he was from Detroit;
Mahoney from a housing project
in South Boston
made sure everyone he met
knew it;
me a farm boy from the corner
of NW Massachusetts
(and embarrassed by that)
we smoked a joint while
we waited for the #10 bus
the streetlights of Boston
glaring,
cans of Budweiser in our pockets--
Mahoney was deaf in one ear
and talked loud enough for everyone on the
bus to hear,
but did not care;
he was a loud-mouth worth listening to
said things worth hearing
—*write about what you know about*—
—*a bad childhood is relevant*—
whenever I asked him to read poems
I wrote
he always made two piles—
good and less good

one day he said *big improvement*
and I felt as if I'd won a prestigious award...
Steinman wrote without use of
punctuation,
between words the
white spaces
where
he lived
in pauses,
mysteries
large and vacant,
like the lawns of
Gross Pointe.

The Track

I know why Bukowski went to the
racetrack so often:
to be around other people—
be near but
not of
humanity;
and then
return to his typewriter and
cigars
and ubiquitous bottle of
whatever
in his room
alone
a misanthrope and
hater of the herd—
like a god who despises
the material
he works with.

4.

emptiness makes the

bowl

useful

Dick at the Fair

Yeah
we was there
my wife and I
she was still alive
'68, '69, must have been
they had these pop guns
you get five shots for a dollar
knock the pigeon off the
wire
my wife hit one dead center
it did not even budge
they must have nailed them down
my wife was ready to shoot
the guy
oh she was mad,
you did not want to rile her
she'd a killed you,
threw a knife at me
once,
parted my hair—
she beat-up two guys in a DENNY'S
one night
then got into a fight with the cops
I had to go to the station
bail her out
I should have left her,
hell

the cops begged me to come get her
she told me they put her into a straight-jacket
I don't know if it is true
they could not stop her from
talking though
she talked more then anyone
I ever knew,
like the radio—
you think I talk a lot
hoo-boy, you should have heard her,
could not get a word in edgewise
I got so sick of listening
one day I pulled the car over,
got out, and
took a cab home,
she had to walk back,
had no money with her,
I laid low after that
did not dare make a peep;
slept in the garage
with the light on...
What was it I started to say,
anyway?
Something about the Fair,
wasn't it?

Dick Puts the Plug in the Jug

I used to go to the dances
at the grange
and before the dance
I would drink wine
4 or 5 pints worth and
I could still navigate
or so I thought
until one night I come out of a black-out
driving a car
at a high rate of speed
and in the rear view mirror
I see blue lights of a cop car
and then I realize they are shooting at me
and boy!
I knew I was in trouble:
I did not have a license.
Hell, I did not own a car either.
They put my picture in the newspaper
afterwards and
I became a marked man
to the cops
so moved
to another state
and soon I found out they had cops there
too
and pretty soon those cops knew me
so I moved again

this time to the city
where I got a room in a rooming house—
the kind of room where
if one cockroach died,
six came to its funeral…
I got a job moving furniture
but
could not keep it
because
once I started drinking
I would forget about working;
I remember coming-to once while sitting
up on the side of my bed
and not knowing
if I was putting my sock on to go out
or taking it off to go to bed—
that is how bad I got—
I wound-up at a drying-out joint
half a dozen times
before I finally
put the plug
in the jug
and kept it there.

Rabies

I am standing on my porch
when I hear kids
screaming
and then a woman
and I run
down the steps and
into the backyard
and jump the fence
into a field
where
this woman
is on top of a fox,
holding it down,
two kids are up in a tree,
I jump on the fox and
try and snap its neck
but cannot do it,
only pisses it off,
its eyes are crazy,
I choke it out
my hands around its throat,
and then a cop
shows up
and I tell him
shoot it

and he says, *geez, I have not used my gun
in a long time,*
and then
takes it out the
holster and shoots
twice,
and the two kids
the mother and me
have to get rabies shots.

The Human Race

after my mother died
the bank took over the house
and threw me out
and I lived in my truck
until my brother let me
stay at his place
but
it did not work out;
my brother is a dink
since he gave up drinking
and started to think
he is better than the rest of us…
Then I found this room,
it ain't a bad place
they give you a free meal
and George,
he is the owner,
ain't a bad guy,
he don't bother you none—
there are ten of us,
two bathrooms;
we get along alright
most of the time—
hey,
why don't we have a drink
for old times' sake?
Or are you too good
too
for the human race?

Ha*

I fought under the name *Kid Berkie*
out of Sullivan's Gym in Tampa, Florida
my trainer, Hector
told me that he once fought
Carmen Basilio and
maybe he did,
maybe not;
he said, *hook to the body,*
like it was a mantra with him
like it was the only English he knew
I said *fuck you, Heck-tor, tell*
me something different,
but he never did
I took an awful beating
my final fight
that fuck Jones
hit me with punches that had not yet been
invented and
I came-to
on the canvas some guy
I did not recognize
waving his arm
like a priest throwing holy water on me
7! 8! 9!...
I am glad I did it,

glad too I quit it;
I get a lot of headaches lately—
bet the guys I fought get them
too.

*"Ha" in medical terminology = headache.

Another Day

they find me sitting up
in my chair
on the back porch
mid-afternoon
gray sky
no visitors for weeks,
maybe more;
my head back
mouth open
eyes pecked-out by birds,
holy shit, a cop says.
I hear him clear as day
I can see him too,
eyes or no eyes,
I am in the sky
above the old ash tree,
seems I can fly,
or something
holds me up,
don't know what,
it is odd
like the sun
setting
in the east
red
like the blanket
the cops
threw over my face.

6.

in Croutonville everyone is guilty
until they prove themselves innocent;
the bums gather in the park,
and hot-rodders roar up and down
the empty streets;
dogs bark at all hours of
the spot-lit nights,
and the primary cause of death
is *O.D.*

I Write for the Factory Workers

the bums,
the burn-outs
the renegades who
left town and never returned;
the unmarried
the unheralded,
lumpen and prole who
never made the honor roll
in High School
never were handed a job
or a promotion
or a trophy,
but got probation,
parole,
an eviction notice,
a Dear John letter,
a court summons,
a pink slip,
a knuckle sandwich,
a room in a nut house,
a ride in the paddy wagon,
a jail sentence,
divorce papers,
bad acid,
food poisoning,

herpes simplex,
crabs,
bronchitis,
mononucleosis,
and hangovers that
lasted for days.

Hypnopompic

after an hour of sleep
alone
in a motel bed
I felt something crawl over my arm
and woke
and on the wall
beyond the other side of the bed
a hairy armed spider
big as a diner plate;
I turned the light on
got up
out of bed
and
carrying a thick paperback book
went to look
for the thing
but could not find
behind the lamp stand
or underneath
or on the floor,
did it go under the bed?
Told myself I would stay awake all night
with the light on
but
became sleepy
so
wrapped a blanket around my head

and lay face-down
and then
thought
how could I have seen the spider in the dark?
Soon
I was asleep
and dreaming
of a guy who
caught spiders and
kept them as pets.

Excavation

digging poems out of a 4-foot high stack
of drafts
to try and revive ones
that almost made it,
close but no cigar:
digging down seven years
to my triple bypass
the bloody remnants
of that trip under lights
the doc and other spacemen
and women in blue scrubs, masks
wheeled me into the
cold operating room,
administered the anesthetic;
I woke in the dark,
a death crypt of some kind
it seemed—in bed with a tube
stuck into my chest,
an iron-curtain ahead
moved back & forth
like fate…
Two nurses told me
get up
out of bed
I said, *I can't*
one said, *yes you can*
they made me stand

and walk
to a chair
in a corner
where I sat
and stared out at
the strange world,
a taste of blood
in my mouth,
and wondering when
my next pill was due.

Reunion

when the family reunion party
breaks-up
I head to DENNY'S
for the brown décor
beige curtains
a waitress I have never seen before
and unknown, to me
characters in separate booths
none of whom ask me
how are you doing?
how is your health?
are you still writing?
The lights above are
truck tire-sized
and a character in the
booth beside me has
his grizzled face in a newspaper;
the waitress is the only one
I have to answer to
though a muscled-up black guy
in a corner stares at me
until I stare back…
The hash browns are
dead on arrival, the
eggs in need of resuscitation

and I have been given toast
not the biscuit I ordered, but
so what? I am in a booth of my
own, a home away from home
until I leave; and
alone
as I need to be.

Nap

slept lying on my back in the
parking lot
behind the Credit Union
under fierce blue clouds
thick as pillows
and full of rain
that never came—
no one run over me
or beat my head in
the tar warm against my
skin
the curb stone a hard cushion
but welcome one;
I woke to the sound of big
trucks up on the highway
their baffles
a stuttering beat of
drum.

1st Book

since my book was
published
I feel as if I have grown
an inch or two,
added an additional foot to my
intestines;
more hair,
harder fingernails,
a darker shadow;
the future has more substance,
I want to hurry it
into existence;
but I fear too
that
it will all end
abruptly
and I will be on my back
in a hospital bed
in Marsailles or
somewhere
and still
unilluminated.

Glucose

the nurse who looks like an
aerobics instructor
wakes me
and I give her my hand
so that she can prick my finger
and check my blood sugar
I am having glucose
pumped into me
via IV
because of diabetes
I never knew I had
until the doc did a chem stick on me
and got a reading of 400
which is high
high
no wonder so thirsty all the time—
why I pissed eight times a night—
my mother's side of the family
loaded with diabetics,
almost as many as the
alcoholics.

7.

words on the hit list:

albeit

kudos

nonplussed

eschew

Loopy

got back with an old girlfriend
the blonde
she came over to my place and
we wound-up making-out on the
bed, her
tits still big, one tit still bigger than the
other; she started to talk crazy,
a paranoid rap that scared me
and I got up, out of bed
no longer interested in sex
and asked her to leave
(told her get a therapist)
and she did leave:
the next day called me five times
but I did not answer;
she lives alone in a house her ex-husband
left half-done while remodeling,
a real mess, no heat
because the furnace broken,
I gave her my space heater,
and this morning
it snowed
but the snow
did not stick.

Raindrops

on the eaves
sound like a beautiful
loneliness,
the only sound
besides her
talking
in the darkened room,
high on medication
or on…
whatever.

The rain drops sound better
than she does.

The Old Lady

I asked the wife to blow me.
She said
blow yourself
I said
I can't
she said
then get one of your girlfriends to do it
I said
I don't have any you bitch
she laughed bitterly
said
who do you think you are fooling?

I wondered how much she knew and
how she knew it—
I said
why would I have a girlfriend with you
around, honey?
She said
I don't know MISTER, you tell me.

I hated that *Mister*
hated those black knee-high boots she
wore
too
(they always meant trouble for me).

She stamped her foot and
threw her mane of auburn hair around
like a prima-donna racehorse in the gate
at Saratoga.
She said
do not think you are getting away with anything
Mister! I can see right through you!

I asked the wife if she was comfortable
she said yes
as comfortable as I can be around you
I said
what does that mean
she said
figure it out yourself
I said
you bitch, I should
she said
should what?
I said I don't know what
she said
how about you should wise-up a little?
I said
how about you should shut-up, a little
she said
don't tell me *shut-up* who do you
think I am, one of your bimbos?
I said
my BIMBOS, oh boy, you have really lost it!
She said
you think?

I said
yeah, you are gonzo, way out there…
She said
and how about you? Do you think you are *normal*?
I said
I never said I was
(whatever *normal* means)
she said
it means not you
I said
oh, it means you though, right?
She said
more so than you.
I said
do you know how idiotic you sound?
She said
me? Oh brother! You are something!
Said
people see through you from a mile away
and you don't even know it!
I said
what the hell you talking about?
She said
wouldn't you like to know?
I said
yeah, I would.
She said
I bet you would
MISTER.

Sunrise at the Sunset

6 AM and the sun
rising
I told the wife *get up*
but she rolled over
started to saw another
log
I saved my breath,
got up, OOB
made some coffee
and took a cup out
to the deck and
the gold fire of sun
sparkling a channel
like a chalice
across the blue ocean,
and the people next door
nowhere in sight
after they were up
blabbering
half the night
(may they die in their sleep)
the wife finally rose,
like the sun, a little
but not shining,
and unfit for company
until after her first
cigarette and cup of coffee.

Spit

she spit into her hand
before she pulled on
my whang
and I thought
wtf? And
started to lose
interest and
then she stuck her tongue
into my ear
and I said
to myself
enough!
and I rolled over
to the far edge of the bed
and stayed
until I heard her
snoring
and felt the ripples of heat
off her body,
like off the pavement on
a hot summer
night.

8.

misty mountain

fa

away

a long long

run

RNA

topaz-green ocean waves
rolling in slow motion
as they have done since
shortly after the earth was formed
and came into being
as somewhere along the line,
some way,
we came to being too
out of a warm soupy puddle
they say
an accident
like when Sally met Harry
and a permeable membrane
formed then all the rest
from microorganism to
Adam
Eve
Nebuchadnezzar
Houdini
Cellini
you,
and *apres vous,*
moi.

Gulf Coast

fierce waves thrashing
shore ward,
like armies of the Great Khan,
butt against the sandy sea wall
which always gives
but never falls;
the bucking steeds retreat
and another line plunges
and wastes itself
in foamy splatter
as I walk past
along the beach
feeling like Caliban
the first man,
or maybe just best known
after Adam—
I sit where Robinson Crusoe sat
with his man, Friday
a big help
(covered the jungle at
Crusoe's back)
Sunday was same as Monday for them
Tuesday not so hot,
always waves flopping
and mad gods in the sky
a horizon full of shark,
'snivilization and savage,

how Crusoe know he no go
into Friday's pot?
An 18th century bromance
or soul-mance
or Rimbaudian farce;
did Crusoe forget what girls looked like?
A left-handed wife,
Rosey Palm and her five sisters
for diversion,
for fun,
if you can call it that
(I can't).

Greatness

sometimes the colorless and dull
break-out the shell and
do something great,
look at Roger Maris,
his 61 home runs
in '61,
after he died
no one remembered him
saying
a noteworthy or memorable
thing;
they only remembered that
besides the homers,
he liked to eat a lot…
Look at Hack Wilson,
his 1930 season.
54 homers, 190 RBI's
a 5' 6" stub, cut by
John McGraw
genius *so-called* manager of the Giants,
he dealt Hack to the Cubs
managed by Joe McCarthy who
handled Hack with kid-gloves—
Hack oversensitive and insecure
(who wouldn't be with dead mother and
father a drunk who lived in a rooming house?)
Hack's 54 homers stood as record 84 years.

When prick Rajah Hornsby replaced McCarthy
Hack began to slide and
slipped out the major leagues after
ten-year career and
died in Baltimore, age 48
alone and broke
but
hell,
for one shining year
he was, like Maris
best in the business.

Soups & Greens

salt & pepper shaker,
empty plate and
cup,
sugar in a bowl,
Ma & Pa Kettle
get up
totter out
the home fries are hard
the waitress has left me
on my own
the Doobie Brothers sing
minute by minute by...
it is Holy Week
and I need to rise
get up
and pay the check
then go back
outside
to whatever
is out there.

Dublin

an arbor in the shade
away from the city noise
and heat,
a silent homeless woman
with her bags,
bird's tweet from the trees;
a guy in gray t-shirt
and baseball cap on backwards
glides in on a bicycle,
his radio playing pop music,
in his hand
a can of Guinness stout
he pours into a cup;
he walks in small circles
like waiting anxiously for the bus,
a sweat-stain shaped like Ireland
on his back.

The birds continue to tweet
but not as sweetly
as before.

One Dog Then

two
then three
in the bark of
early morning,
then the roosters
the roofers
next door
their radio turned up
loud
then cars
going-by and
multiplying;
the alien voice
of the radio
speaks to the neighborhood
but not to me
sitting in a doorway
on the 2nd floor
across the way,
warm sun on
my cold flesh.

Budapest

I stopped in an alleyway
in the city
to look at stacks of paintings
by a guy
who sat nearby
he asked me where I was from
I said *Czechoslovakia*
just to fuck with him,
he said, *I am from Budapest,*
I said, *no shit*, and
then picked out a painting:
how much?
$120, he said,
but with Slovakian discount, $60.
I bought it.

Eye

a shag carpet of
golden leaves mixed
with brown
my brother and me
rake into a pile
and dive in:
the next month
November
the ground turns hard
but we continue to play
football
in the yard
and I get a lump of earth
into my eye socket
when I go down
and the socket swells and
turns black then brown
and I wear dark glasses to
school
and kids call me *movie star*
and ask to see the eye
which I show
every once in a while

if in the mood.

Last Bus

a snowfall in Dublin
and people from the pubs
are in the street
throwing snowballs
at a cop
and everyone laughs
even the cop,
who loses his cap,
and I hurry past
dark doorways
full of groping couples
and to the bus stop
to catch the bus so that
I do not have to walk back
to my room,
a cold basement flat
in Drumcondra.

Meanwhile

I go into Cumberbund Farms
to buy a newspaper.
A catchy pop-tune on the
radio,
a fat girl
at the ATM machine
gives me the eye;
Steve makes change of
my sawbuck
as a short-guy
behind me
exudes an aura of menace
hard to ignore…
Out by the pumps
pretty girls
get in
get out
of cars
(but do not come inside).
Thin roadside trees with buds
on their branches
sway in the breeze.

8.

life is good when you

have no pain

but who

hoo

has no pain?

Door-Knob

walking through well-lit hallways of
an apartment building trying door knobs
until one turns
and I walk into
a dark room
faintly lit
by streetlights
other rooms
also dark,
a back room
and a girl
lying on a mattress
on the floor
I kneel and massage her
bare back,
she stirs and moans
contentedly;
a gust of wind sweeps-up the
window curtain and
it or something else
calls me elsewhere
and I leave,
wander city streets
who knows how long or
where

before I am back at the door
only now locked
and as I tug the knob
the curtain in the window
is swept aside
and a girl, eyes stark
stares back
terrified.

In Case of Emergency

I spent days in the streets of the
city and
nights sleeping on a bench in
Longfellow Park
(some fucking poet he must have been)
and woke with the back of my head
flat as the bench.

I drank whiskey to help me,
to sleep and
for other reasons;
tried to keep one eye open
as I slept:
had a job
but
like Jesus,
nowhere to lay my head,
except the bench,
because
no rooms in the city
to rent until
one night
a room opened up at the Y
and I filled the preregistration form
but
after told by the clerk
to fill in the space

in case of emergency notify
I crumpled it up and
threw it at him across
the desk
because
well,
who in hell was he
tell me what to do?

Later,
back on my bench,
I told myself
I must be nuts.

Shut-Off

it had been a good day
until two cruisers moved-in
and cut me off
in the crosswalk,
a sunny afternoon
in the city,
one cop threw me
onto the hood of the car
another hand-cuffed me.

Me, the *unidentified man*
in the newspaper story
of the morning edition.

The cops knew who I was
but I didn't.

The bartender knew that
I did not need another drink
but I knew I did and
after he shut me off
I climbed over the bar
and made my own,
and when he slapped the drink
from my hand
I punched him and
ran out

and became *unidentified*
for a day
or two, until cops
closed in
at the intersection of
State and Main.

It a Lie

a lie
I will never
die
I will never
be in need
never cry
at night
not me
not me
I am
different
breed of
liar.

Wayne F. Burke was born in 1954 in a small manufacturing town in the North Berkshire Hills of Massachusetts. His father, Edward, had been a sergeant in the Marine Corp before becoming manager of a Mobil Flying-A Gasoline station; his mother, Claire Burke nee Kelly, had worked in a textile mill before becoming a full-time housewife. Both of his parents died young: his mother at twenty-eight--at which time his father moved him and his three siblings to the home of the paternal grandparents. His father died at thirty-two. The four children were raised by the grandparents and an Uncle. The grandfather was owner and operator of BURKE'S INN, a generational business begun previous to the First World War. Wayne F. Burke attended public school, and after graduating from High School, three institutions of higher learning before graduating from Goddard College in 1979 (B.A. RUP). After graduation he traveled around the country, living in a variety of places and working at a variety of occupations (presently, he is employed as an LPN in a nursing home). In the late-80's he located himself in the central Vermont area and has remained since. He published mostly prose until 2013 when his first poetry collection was published. He was fifty-eight years old. ESCAPE FROM THE PLANET CROUTON is his 7th published poetry collection. A book of short stories, titled TURMOIL & Other Stories, is scheduled for publication by Adelaide Press in 2020.

www.ingramcontent.com/pod-product-compliance
Lightning Source LLC
Chambersburg PA
CBHW022009120526
44592CB00034B/763